WILLIAM HENRY Harrison

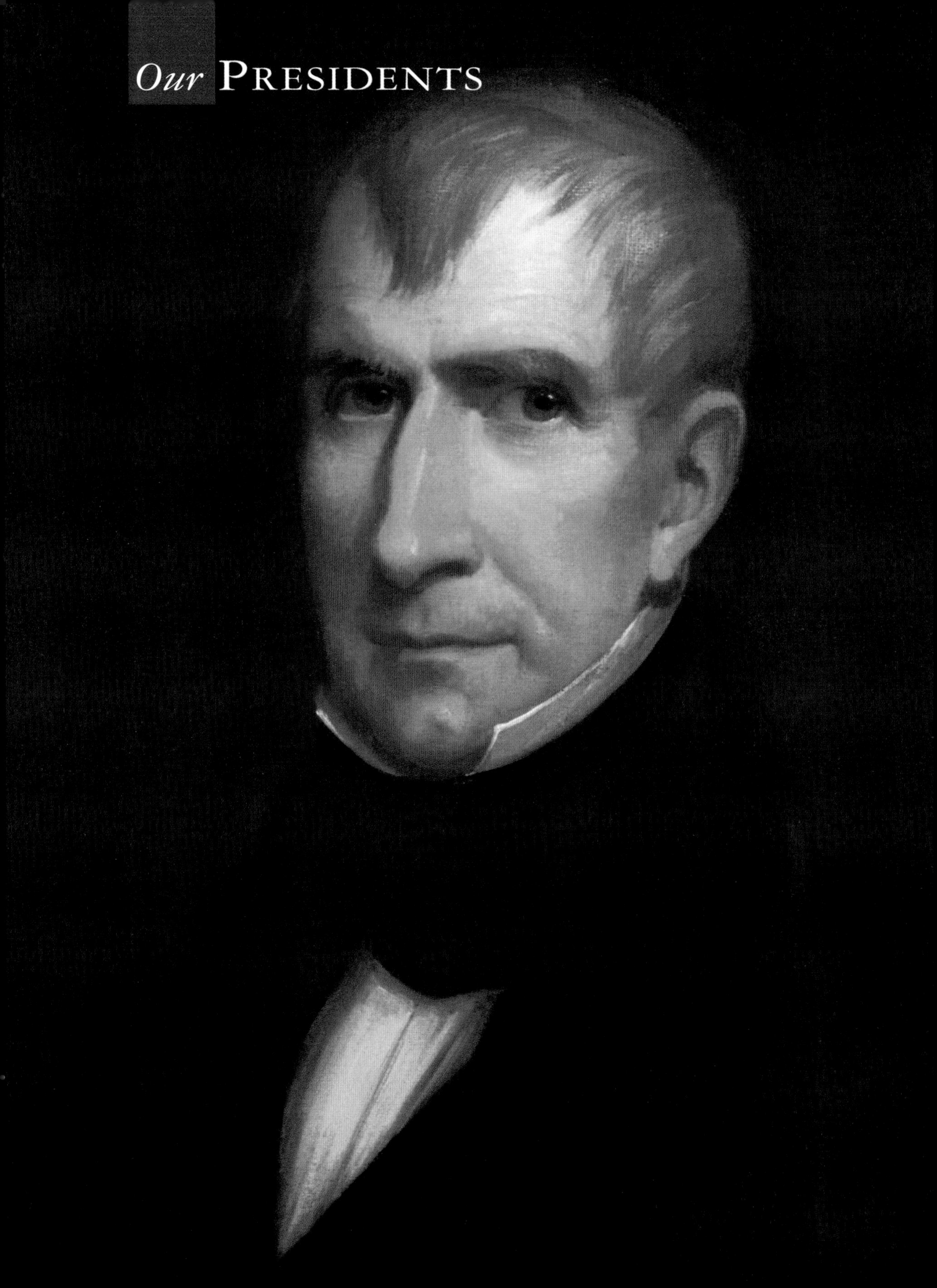

William Henry *Harrison*

By Ann Graham Gaines

SPIRIT
of America™

The Child's World®, Inc.
Chanhassen, Minnesota

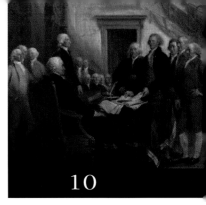
10

WILLIAM HENRY *Harrison*

Published in the United States of America by The Child's World®, Inc.
PO Box 326 • Chanhassen, MN 55317-0326 • 800-599-READ • www.childsworld.com

Acknowledgments

The Creative Spark: Mary Francis-DeMarois, Project Director; Elizabeth Sirimarco Budd, Series Editor; Robert Court, Design and Art Direction; Janine Graham, Page Layout; Jennifer Moyers, Production

The Child's World®, Inc.: Mary Berendes, Publishing Director; Red Line Editorial, Fact Research; Cindy Klingel, Curriculum Advisor; Robert Noyed, Historical Advisor

Photos

Cover: White House Collection, courtesy White House Historical Association; Courtesy of the Benjamin Harrison Home, Indianapolis, Indiana: 6, 7, 8, 12, 13, 14, 27, 28, 33; Courtesy of Berkeley Plantation, Charles City, Virginia: 7; Chicago Historical Society P&S-1971.0177, Artist: Alonzo Chappel; Corbis: 16, 23, 31; © Francis G. Mayer/Corbis: 10; The Granger Collection, New York: 9, 15, 19, 21; Courtesy of The Hermitage: 26; The Library of Congress: 22, 24, 29, 30, 35; National Portrait Gallery, Smithsonian Institution, Art Resource, NY: 20; Stock Montage: 18; White House Collection, courtesy White House Historical Association, 37 except portrait of John F. Kennedy, courtesy of Jamie Wyeth

Registration

The Child's World®, Inc., Spirit of America™, and their associated logos are the sole property and registered trademarks of The Child's World®, Inc.

Library of Congress Cataloging-in-Publication Data

Gaines, Ann.
  William Henry Harrison : our ninth president / by Ann Graham Gaines.
    p. cm.
    Includes bibliographical references and index.
  ISBN 1-56766-848-8 (lib. bdg. : alk. paper)
  1. Harrison, William Henry, 1773–1841—Juvenile literature. 2. Presidents—United States—
Biography—Juvenile literature. [1. Harrison, William Henry, 1773–1841. 2. Presidents.] I. Title.
  E392 .G35 2001
  973.8'6'092—dc21
                                                        00-011452

Contents

Chapter ONE

Early Days

William Henry Harrison was the nation's ninth president. He had the misfortune of being the first president to die in office.

WHEN WILLIAM HENRY HARRISON RAN FOR president in the election of 1840, he told Americans he was from "out West." He and his supporters claimed that he lived in a log cabin. They hoped everyone would believe he was a brave pioneer, someone who had settled on the wild frontier of America—the very edge of settled lands. They did not want people to know that he came from a rich and powerful family from the East.

William Henry Harrison was born on a large farm, called a plantation, in Charles County, Virginia. His birthday was February 9, 1773. Benjamin and Elizabeth Harrison, his parents, had seven children. William Henry was the youngest. The Harrison family lived a luxurious life. Their home was a mansion

with 22 rooms, each one filled with fancy furniture. The children did not go to school because their family was wealthy enough to hire a tutor. This special teacher taught them at their home.

Benjamin Harrison was a planter, a person who owns a plantation. He earned money selling crops that were raised on his farm.

William Henry Harrison was born at Berkeley Plantation, the beautiful estate that his grandfather built in 1726. It is located in Virginia on the James River. George Washington and each of the next nine presidents visited the plantation.

7

But he did not actually do farm work. Instead, he owned many slaves. They worked in his fields growing tobacco, cotton, and vegetables. Slaves did all the work in the Harrisons' house, too. They cooked, cleaned, and even sewed clothing for the family.

Benjamin Harrison was also involved in politics, the work of the government. When William Henry was born, his father had been a member of Virginia's **legislature** for 24 years. The legislature wrote laws for Virginia, which was then one of the 13 British colonies.

The American Revolution began when William Henry was two years old. The American colonies fought this war to win their independence from Great Britain. It would not end for six difficult years. Harrison thought it was exciting to grow up during the Revolution. He liked to watch soldiers march by and hear bands play patriotic songs.

Benjamin Harrison, William Henry's father, started the family tradition of entering politics. He was the governor of Virginia for three terms.

8

Americans know that the Pilgrims and Native Americans held a feast of thanksgiving together in Plymouth (in what is now Massachusetts). This is often called the first Thanksgiving. But other similar celebrations were held by colonists in other places. One was held even earlier on land owned by William Henry Harrison's ancestors.

Benjamin Harrison was a **patriot.** In 1775, he left Virginia's legislature after he was elected to the Continental Congress. During and after the Revolution, the Continental Congress governed all the colonies. Its members met in Philadelphia, Pennsylvania. This kept Benjamin Harrison away from home for long periods of time. In 1776, the Continental Congress asked Thomas Jefferson to write the **Declaration of Independence.** When he finished, all the members of Congress signed it, including Benjamin Harrison. The Declaration of Independence said a new country was born— the United States of America.

Benjamin Harrison went back to his plantation after the American Revolution ended.

9

Benjamin Harrison, William Henry's father, was one of the men who signed the Declaration of Independence. This important document officially created a new nation—the United States of America.

There he continued as a member of Virginia's legislature until he was elected governor of the state. The Harrison children liked having their father home again after the war was over. While Benjamin was away, the family's tutor had taught William Henry to read and write. He also taught mathematics and languages such as Greek and Latin. William Henry learned about politics and government from his father. He was a smart boy. By the time he was 15, he was ready to enroll at Hampden-Sydney College in Virginia.

William Henry did not stay at the college long enough to graduate. He decided he wanted to become a doctor instead. In 1790, he left Hampden-Sydney College to attend medical school. Soon he realized he did not want a career in medicine after all. William Henry returned to Hampden-Sydney College, but not for long. After Benjamin Harrison died in 1791, William Henry left school for good. He had decided to become a soldier.

On August 16, 1791, at age 18, he joined the army as an officer, a person who commands soldiers in the army. There was no war at the time, however. The army's main responsibility was to protect settlers on the frontier from Native American attacks. Sometimes groups of Native Americans killed settlers or burned their houses. What the Native Americans really wanted to do was scare the settlers away. They wanted to take back the land that had belonged to them for centuries.

11

Harrison **recruited** 80 other men to join the army. They formed a company of soldiers, which he commanded. The army ordered Harrison and his men to march west over the Allegheny Mountains to a fort on the Ohio River. Today the city of Cincinnati, Ohio, is located there.

Harrison was a soldier in the army for almost seven years. He and his men built new forts. They also fought Native Americans at times. Harrison was a brave man who was skilled at shooting a gun and commanding soldiers.

While in the army, Harrison met Anna Symmes. In 1795, they married. Anna's father feared that Harrison would not make a good husband because he was a soldier. He worried that Harrison's work was too risky and that he might be killed one day. But the Harrisons' marriage was a happy one. They had 10 children in 19 years. Unfortunately, six of their children died while they were still young.

In 1798, Harrison left the army. He wanted to become a farmer, but he and his wife did not want to move to his home state of Virginia to live. They wanted to stay on the frontier. So Harrison bought 160 acres of land

Anna Symmes Harrison was as independent as her husband. When her parents refused to let her marry William Henry, she decided to elope. Over the years, her husband was often away, so she cared for the family and home by herself.

to farm. It was located on the Ohio River, 14 miles south of where Cincinnati is today.

Farming was not all Harrison planned to do, however. Now 25 years old, he had many goals. Most of all, he wanted to become a powerful **politician** like his father had been.

The Harrisons built a lovely home on their land, which overlooked the Ohio River.

Chapter TWO

Life in Indiana

Harrison began his career in politics in 1798 when he was named the secretary of the Northwest Territory. It was the first of many positions he would hold in his lifetime.

AFTER THE AMERICAN REVOLUTION, SOME states that are small today were actually quite big. Connecticut, Massachusetts, and New York all owned land to the west. These lands stretched as far as the Mississippi River. All three states gave up most of their western land to the **federal** government in the 1780s.

In 1787, Congress passed the Northwest Ordinance. This law made the government's new western lands into the Northwest **Territory.** The ordinance said that when the population became large enough, the territory could break up into smaller territories. Then those territories could become new states. More and more settlers moved into these areas over the next 10 years. Some people became farmers. Others opened stores and

The Northwest Ordinance of 1787 created a new territory in the West. It stretched all the way to the Mississippi River.

offices in new towns that were founded all around the territory.

Harrison began a long career in politics on June 29, 1798. Congress named him the secretary of the Northwest Territory. His job was to keep records for the government. In 1799, he left that position. He was elected the Territory's **representative** to the U.S. Congress. Harrison left his family behind and went to Philadelphia, then the nation's capital.

In Congress, he often spoke up for westerners. He wanted to make sure they got their share of the federal government's money. He wanted roads and waterways built in the West, not just in the East. One of Harrison's most important achievements while in Congress was introducing the Land Act of 1800. This law lowered the price families paid to buy small plots of land in the West. It meant more people could move to the frontier and begin new lives.

In 1800, Congress passed a law that divided the Northwest Territory. Harrison became governor of one part, which became the territory of Indiana. He and his family then went to live in Vincennes, the capital of Indiana at the time. He remained governor for 12 years, from January of 1801 to December of

Thousands of settlers traveled into the Northwest Territory to set up homesteads. They were excited at the prospect of starting new lives on the frontier. Harrison wanted to help these settlers. He passed a law that lowered the price of land in the West.

1812. He helped establish the territory's legislature and chose other officials to help him run the new government.

The biggest problem that Harrison faced as governor was the Native Americans. Settlers wanted to take over more and more Native American land. Harrison knew the settlers were taking away the Native Americans' rights. They were also treating them poorly. But Harrison finally decided that the rights of settlers, not those of the Native Americans, were his responsibility. As governor, he met with Native American chiefs. He convinced leaders to give up their land to the American government. Sometimes the government paid the Native Americans for their land, but it never gave them very much money.

In 1809, Harrison **negotiated** the Treaty of Fort Wayne, an agreement between the United States and many different Native American tribes. The Delaware, Miami, Potawatomi, and Eel tribes agreed to give the United States three million acres of land. The government agreed to pay each tribe a few hundred dollars a year for a certain amount of time.

Interesting Facts

▶ William Henry Harrison was the first congressman ever elected from Indiana. He was also the first governor of Indiana.

Settlers on the frontier had violent disagreements with Native Americans. The United States wanted to control more and more of the continent. The government did not care that Native Americans had lived on the land for centuries.

Many Native Americans did not like what was happening. Some British people living in Canada encouraged the Native Americans to fight the settlers. Two brothers named Tecumseh and Tenskwatawa belonged to the Shawnee tribe. They wanted to help Native Americans end what they believed was as an invasion by white people. Tecumseh formed a **confederation** of tribes. He convinced Native American people from as far away as Canada and Florida to join forces. Fighting together, they would have a better chance in battles against the settlers. Tenskwatawa, whom Americans called "The Prophet," tried to help Native Americans bring back their **traditions.** He wanted them to stop buying goods such as rifles and alcohol from white people. He said they should live as their ancestors had.

Together, the members of Tecumseh's confederation owned a great deal of land. Harrison tried to get Tecumseh to agree to sell the government their land in Indiana. He offered $10,000, but Tecumseh refused. He told Harrison that "the Americans had driven them from the sea coast." What Tecumseh meant was that his people had been pushed out of places such as Virginia and Massachusetts by white settlers. Tecumseh predicted that Americans "would shortly, if not stopped, push them into the [Great] Lakes."

Tecumseh began to bring together a large group of warriors. He was trying to build a powerful Native American army. These warriors built a town on Tippecanoe Creek.

Tenskwatawa, known as "The Prophet," led Native American warriors in the Battle of Tippecanoe.

Settlers were fearful of what would happen next. In 1811, they asked Harrison to take action against Tecumseh and his warriors. Harrison led 800 soldiers into battle, even though he was still the governor. He said he planned to deal the tribes "a sweeping blow," by destroying their town by the creek.

But before the Americans reached the Native Americans' town, Tenskwatawa launched a surprise attack early in the morning. (Tecumseh was not there. He had gone off to recruit more warriors.)

Westerners believed the Battle of Tippecanoe was a great victory against the Native Americans. Harrison's actions made him a hero to people all around the country. The battle was so famous in the United States that Harrison was nicknamed "Old Tippecanoe."

Interesting Facts

▶ Tecumseh, whose name means "Cougar Crouching for His Prey," was a Shawnee Indian chief known as a fierce warrior. Once he arrived at a battle just in time to see Native Americans brutally killing their American prisoners. Tecumseh scolded the warriors and stopped the violence. This incident strengthened the great chief's reputation among Native Americans and Americans alike.

"Indians were in the Camp before many of my men could get out of their tents," Harrison later wrote. Sixty-one American soldiers died and 127 were wounded in the Battle of Tippecanoe. Many Native Americans died as well. Finally, the tribes were forced to flee. The U.S. soldiers who were not hurt in battle moved on to burn the Native American village. With that, they could claim a victory, and Harrison was a hero.

20

BEFORE THE BATTLE OF TIPPECANOE, THE SHAWNEE AMERICAN INDIANS HAD attacked whites who moved onto their lands for many years. Tecumseh, whose father had been a war chief, fought in his first battle when he was just nine years old. By the time he was 20, he had become famous not only as a fierce warrior, but also as an intelligent man. He knew many Native American languages, as well as English and French.

Tecumseh traveled hundreds of miles east of the Mississippi River, forming a confederation of Native American tribes. He explained that tribes had to protect their way of life, or it would be destroyed forever. To do this, every tribe had to join together. Many Native Americans accepted him as their leader. His confederation eventually included 50 tribes. They promised to stop fighting each other and to fight the Americans together.

Tecumseh built a powerful Native American army. It fought on the side of the British in the War of 1812. In exchange, the British promised that they would give the Native Americans what is now Michigan at the end of the war. But this did not happen. Tecumseh died at the Battle of the Thames on October 5, 1813. The alliance broke up after his death.

Chapter THREE

A Long Political Life

Harrison was named a general after the Battle of Tippecanoe. Generals are the most important officers in the army.

AFTER THE BATTLE OF TIPPECANOE, THE WHITE settlers of Indiana considered Harrison a hero. So did most Americans in other places. A well-known congressman named Henry Clay wrote to Harrison, saying that he admired him and his courage. In the years that followed, Clay became Harrison's friend and helped him in his political career. Not all Americans believed Harrison's actions were right, however. Some politicians accused him of "horrible butchery." They said that too many Americans had died in the battle. Unfortunately, few politicians were concerned about the Native American lives that were lost.

Harrison's victory in the Battle of Tippe-canoe did not help Americans solve their problems with Native Americans. In 1812, war broke out between the United States and Great Britain. Tecumseh and his warriors became British **allies,** fighting together against the Americans.

In August of 1812, Governor Harrison joined the army once more. Henry Clay persuaded army officials to make him a general, one of the army's most important commanders. The following year, Clay convinced Congress to give Harrison command of a large group of soldiers, called the Northwestern Army.

Congressman Henry Clay admired Harrison's actions during the Battle of Tippe-canoe. He recommended that the army make Harrison a general and give him more responsibility.

In December of 1812, Harrison's term as governor of Indiana ended. He decided to stay in the army. He fought with all his might during the War of 1812. Twice British soldiers surrounded his men, putting them under **siege.** The Americans could not leave their camp. They became very hungry because they ran out of supplies. Still, they held on. Finally, the British gave up and left them alone.

After the British captured the city of Detroit, Harrison and his men fought fiercely to win it back for the United States. On October 5, 1813, his men beat a large group of Native American warriors and British soldiers in the Battle of the Thames. Tecumseh died in that battle. After his death, the confederation of Native Americans he had founded fell apart. Native Americans no longer challenged American settlers' claim to the northwestern lands.

In May of 1814, Harrison retired from the army. He was 41 years old. Over the next 25

Harrison and his men were victorious at the Battle of the Thames on October 5, 1813. Tecumseh died in the battle. Without the chief's leadership, the Native American confederation fell apart.

years, he tended his farm. He also ran for many political offices, often because he needed the salary the government pays its politicians. It cost Harrison a great deal of money to raise his large family. He also really enjoyed politics. For many years, Harrison belonged to the Democratic **political party,** which had been started years before by Thomas Jefferson and other founding fathers.

From 1816 to 1819, Harrison represented Indiana in Congress. From 1819 to 1821, he served in the Ohio State Senate. His land sat on the border between the territories of Ohio and Indiana, so he could serve in both states. Several times, he ran for election as governor of Ohio, but he never won.

Harrison did win other elections, however. He was a U.S. senator from 1825 to 1828. There he had a very important job. He was in charge of the committee on military affairs. He was also a supporter of the president, John Quincy Adams. In 1828, Adams rewarded Harrison for his loyalty by naming him the **minister** to the South American country of Colombia. The next year, Democrat Andrew Jackson became president. Jackson hated Adams

Interesting Facts

▶ Even after the War of 1812, warfare against Native Americans raged on for many years all around the continent. The United States was determined to control the land from coast to coast.

▶ In 1818, Congress voted to give Harrison a gold medal for the courage he displayed as a soldier in the War of 1812.

▶ Anna Harrison did not want her husband to run for president in the elections of 1836 and 1840. She wanted "Pa," as she called him, to stay home and work the family farm.

and his allies. He took away Harrison's job so he could give it to one of his own supporters.

Harrison returned from Colombia in September of 1829. He returned to the task of tending his farm. He also changed political parties. He was so angry at the way Andrew Jackson had treated him, he left the Democratic Party. He joined the new Whig Party. This political party was formed to oppose Jackson's Democrats.

In 1834, Harrison took a job keeping records for the county court to earn extra money. One year later, he decided to run for the most important office in the nation. He began to **campaign** for the 1836 presidential election. He traveled around Indiana and Illinois talking to voters, trying to get them to vote for him.

That year, Americans celebrated the 25th anniversary of the Battle of Tippecanoe. When people told the story of what had happened there, they described Harrison as a hero. Harrison received the most votes in seven states. But Democrat Martin Van Buren won the election in even more states. He became the president in 1837.

Andrew Jackson was another hero from the War of 1812. When he became president in 1829, he removed all of his political enemies from government positions—including William Henry Harrison. The Whig Party was formed to fight Jackson and his followers.

TODAY PRESIDENTIAL CAMPAIGNS LAST FOR MORE THAN A YEAR. PRESIDENTIAL **candidates** make many public appearances. They give speeches and appear in television commercials. Voters have many chances to find out who the candidates are and what they plan to do if they become president.

George Washington and other early presidents did not campaign. Voters chose presidents based on what they had already accomplished. William Henry Harrison was the first presidential candidate to campaign. He made appearances at dozens of political rallies and picnics. People began calling Harrison "Tippecanoe." Democrats shouted "Tippecanoe and Tyler, Too" at rallies to signal their support for Harrison and the vice presidential candidate, John Tyler. They even wrote songs praising Harrison and Tyler and held parades in their honor. The poster shown here features a log cabin, a symbol of Harrison's campaign.

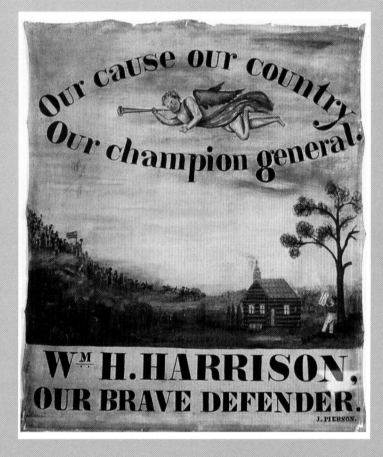

27

Chapter FOUR

The Shortest Presidency

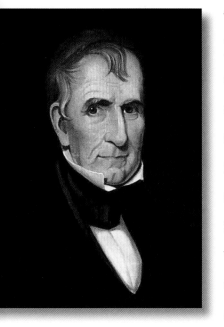

The Whigs were determined to win the election of 1840, and they chose William Henry Harrison as their candidate.

THE WHIGS WERE DISAPPOINTED THAT VAN Buren became the new president. They immediately set to work, planning to win the next election. For years, the Democrats had claimed to be the party of the people. This meant that they represented working people, such as farmers and shopkeepers, instead of rich people. But the Whigs usually helped wealthy businessmen and Southern plantation owners. Now the Whigs realized the votes of ordinary working people were important, too. They wanted to attract the votes of laborers, farmers, and frontiersmen.

Leaders of the Whig Party decided Harrison could beat Van Buren in the next presidential election. They asked Harrison to run and began to create a positive image for

28

him. They praised him as a war hero. To make him seem like a regular person, they said Harrison lived on the frontier in a log cabin. They said he liked to drink hard cider, which is a drink made from apples, instead of expensive wines from foreign countries. The Whigs hoped this would increase Harrison's appeal to ordinary Americans.

Harrison's supporters also told lies about Van Buren. Whig newspaper editors criticized the president. They said Van Buren was a dandy, a man who is too concerned about his appearance. They claimed he loved to look at himself in mirrors!

Americans were arguing over some very big issues. The country was beginning to divide over the issue of whether to outlaw slavery.

During his campaign to become president, William Henry Harrison traveled around the country with a small log cabin and hard cider that he offered to voters. Harrison lived in a mansion on a huge farm, not in a log cabin. But he described his opponent, Martin Van Buren, as someone who lived like a king. He said Van Buren didn't understand the needs of the average American.

Many people who lived in the North wanted it ended in all the states. But Southerners depended on slaves to work on their plantations. They believed ending slavery would ruin their **economy.** Americans also disagreed over tariffs, which are taxes placed on goods brought in from foreign countries. For years, they had been arguing over whether to have a national bank that controlled all the government's money. Some leaders wanted to distribute the money among many smaller banks instead of giving so much power to a single large one.

Whig Party leaders ordered Harrison not to speak out about topics such as slavery, tariffs, and the U.S. bank system. They didn't want him to lose votes by expressing an unpopular opinion.

Harrison traveled all over delivering speeches. People turned out in great numbers for his rallies, which were large celebrations held to show support for him. Harrison easily won the election of 1840.

30

Harrison's inauguration took place on a terribly cold day. Still, he gave a very long speech. In fact, it was the longest inaugural address ever given.

He traveled by train to Washington, D.C., becoming the first president to arrive by rail for his **inauguration.** He was sworn in on March 4, 1841. Anna Harrison was sick when her husband was elected. She could not go to Washington with him at first. Unfortunately, her husband would die before she arrived in the capital city.

The day of Harrison's inauguration was cold and wet. The ceremony took place outside. To get there, Harrison rode a horse. He wore no hat or coat. Then he stood in the icy rain for more than two hours. It took him that long to read his inaugural address, the speech the

▸ When Anna Harrison heard that her husband had been elected president, she said, "I wish that my husband's friends had left him where he is, happy and contented in retirement."

▸ Harrison was the first president to have his picture taken while he was in office. It was an early type of photograph called a daguerreotype.

president gives to the public on inauguration day. The crowd in attendance was larger than any since George Washington had been sworn in some 50 years before.

Later, Harrison went out walking and was caught in a rainstorm. He was drenched and caught a cold. That evening, he said he did not feel very well. But he started to work right away the next morning. Over the next two weeks, he made many political **appointments,** assigning people to important government positions. Thousands of people wrote or came to ask Harrison for a job. "The job seekers pack the White House every day," he said. But he did not want to be a puppet who just did what members of his political party wanted. In fact, Harrison's cabinet, the group of men who helped him make decisions, wanted him to appoint someone he did not respect as the governor of Iowa. Harrison refused to give in to their pressure.

In late March, doctors said the president had **pneumonia** and ordered him to bed. Doctors tried "modern" treatments, such as applying heated cups to his skin to draw out the disease. They even tried traditional Native American cures.

Newspapers did not report that Harrison was sick until March 31. By this time he was very weak, and his wife was still in Ohio. Anna received a message telling her that her husband was sick. But she did not arrive in time to see Harrison before he died on April 4, 1841. His vice president, John Tyler, had also been away. He did not know Harrison died until the next day.

Americans were shocked when newspapers announced the president's death. People gathered

William Henry Harrison died on April 4, a month after his inauguration. His presidency is the shortest in American history.

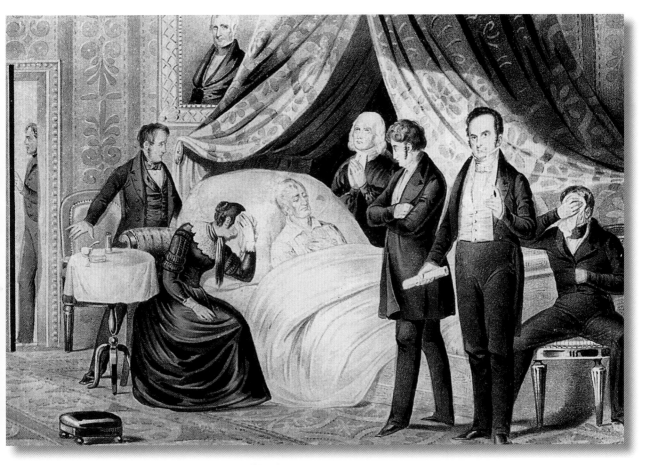

on street corners and in shops to talk about the sad event. They wondered what would happen next. In Washington, businesses and offices shut down. Government buildings were draped in black fabric as a sign of respect and sorrow for the president.

Harrison's body lay at the White House. He was honored with an official funeral. Important people crowded into the East Room of the White House to pay their respects. After officials spoke, men carried out his coffin and placed it on a wagon painted black. A band played dirges, very sad songs that are played at funerals. A large group of people followed the wagon to the Congressional Cemetery. Later that month, Harrison's coffin was taken by train to Ohio, where it was buried.

For a short time, no one was sure what to do. Should the United States swear in a new president right away? Should it wait for a time to show respect for President Harrison? There were also questions about who should become the president. But Vice President Tyler said that he should be made president. He quickly made arrangements to be sworn in.

Tyler's actions created the tradition that has always been followed when an American president dies in office. Today Americans know that there is always a chance the president will die during his term. They count on the government to keep working if this ever happens.

No one knows what kind of president Harrison would have been. Would he have helped his nation? The last words that Harrison spoke were said to his doctor. But perhaps they were meant for the person who would take over leadership. "Sir," said Harrison, "I wish you to understand the true **principles** of the government. I wish them carried out. I ask nothing more."

Portraits of Harrison were made after his death and sold to the American people, who were greatly saddened by his death.

EIGHT AMERICAN PRESIDENTS HAVE DIED IN OFFICE. WILLIAM HENRY Harrison was the first. In 1850, Zachary Taylor (top left, opposite page) became the second president to die during his term. On April 14, 1865, in one of saddest events in American history, Abraham Lincoln (below) was **assassinated.** A Southerner named John Wilkes Booth was angry that the North had won the Civil War. Booth shot Lincoln at a theater, while the president was watching a play. Americans were shocked by the assassination, and they thought such a terrible thing could never happen again. They were wrong.

An insane man who believed he should have been given an important government position shot James Garfield (top center). Garfield died
September 19, 1881. William McKinley (top right) was shot by a man
who wanted to overthrow the government. He died on September 14,
1901. In 1923, Warren G. Harding (bottom left) died from a sudden
illness. Franklin D. Roosevelt (bottom center) served as president longer
than any other. He faced two serious problems that left him frail and
exhausted: the Great Depression and World War II. He died on April
12, 1945, soon after his fourth inauguration. The last president to die in
office was John F. Kennedy (bottom right), who was assassinated on
November 22, 1963. Americans who were alive at the time will never
forget the grief they felt when they heard the news.

1773 William Henry Harrison is born on February 9 on his family's Virginia plantation. His parents, Benjamin and Elizabeth, have seven children.

1775 The American Revolution begins.

1776 Benjamin Harrison, a member of the Continental Congress, signs the Declaration of Independence. The United States is born.

1788 Harrison enrolls at Hampden-Sydney College in Virginia. He is 15 years old.

1787 The U.S. Congress passes the Northwest Ordinance. This law creates the Northwest Territory from the government's western lands. Ohio, Indiana, Illinois, Michigan, and Wisconsin will later be formed out of the Territory.

1790 Harrison leaves college to begin studying medicine.

1791 Harrison decides he does not want to become a doctor. He briefly returns to Hampden-Sydney College before deciding to become a soldier. He joins the army as an officer. The army sends him and his company of soldiers to Ohio to help protect settlers on the frontier.

1795 Harrison marries Anna Symmes, whom he met in Ohio.

1798 On June 1, Harrison resigns from the army. He becomes secretary of the Northwest Territory.

1799 Harrison is elected to the U.S. House of Representatives.

1800 President John Adams appoints Harrison governor of the new Indiana Territory.

1801 Harrison begins his new job as governor of Indiana in January. He holds the position for 12 years.

1809 Harrison negotiates the Treaty of Fort Wayne with the Delaware, Miami, Potawatomi, and Eel Native American tribes. The tribes agree to give the American government millions of acres of their land.

1810 Shawnee Chief Tecumseh starts to build a confederation of Native American tribes. He wants warriors to form an army to force settlers from Native American lands.

1811 Harrison leads soldiers in the Battle of Tippecanoe, against Tecumseh's soldiers, on November 11. The Americans win the battle.

1812 The War of 1812 begins. Harrison rejoins the army, even though he is still governor of Indiana. In December, his term as governor ends.

1813 Harrison is given command of the Northwestern Army. On October 5, he and his men fight the Battle of the Thames. Tecumseh dies in the battle.

1814 In May, Harrison retires from the army and goes home to his farm.

1816 Harrison is again elected to the U.S. House of Representatives.

1819 Harrison leaves the House of Representatives. He is then elected to the Ohio State Senate.

1821 Harrison leaves his seat in the Ohio Senate. He runs for governor of Ohio several times over the next few years but is not elected.

1825 The people of Ohio elect Harrison to the U.S. Senate.

1828 President John Quincy Adams appoints Harrison minister to Colombia, a country in South America. Harrison resigns his seat in the U.S. Senate to accept the position.

1829 Harrison comes home from Colombia. A new president, Andrew Jackson, has given the position to one of his own supporters.

1835 Harrison begins to campaign for the 1836 presidential election. He travels all over the Midwest to meet voters and give speeches.

1836 Harrison is praised as a war hero, but he is not elected president.

1838 Although the next presidential election is still two years away, leaders of the Whig Party discuss how to keep President Van Buren from being reelected. They ask Harrison to run against him.

1839 Harrison campaigns for election as president in what is called the Log Cabin Campaign. His opponent is again Martin Van Buren.

1840 Harrison defeats Martin Van Buren and is elected president.

1841 Harrison is inaugurated on March 4. The day of his inauguration is cold and wet, and he catches a cold. By the end of the month, he is very ill. On April 4, he dies of pneumonia. John Tyler becomes the nation's 10th president.

allies (AL-lize)
Allies are people or nations that have agreed to help each other by fighting together against a common enemy. During the War of 1812, Native Americans were British allies.

appointments (uh-POINT-mintz)
Appointments are important positions in the government to which a person is assigned by an official. President Harrison made political appointments to many positions.

assassinate (uh-SASS-ih-nayt)
Assassinate means to murder someone, especially a well-known person. President Lincoln was assassinated in 1865.

campaign (kam-PAYN)
A campaign is the process of running for an election, including activities such as giving speeches or attending rallies. Harrison was the first presidential candidate to campaign.

candidates (KAN-dih-detz)
Candidates are people running in an election. Presidential candidates make many public appearances.

confederation (kun-fed-er-AY-shun)
A confederation is a group of people who come together for a common purpose. Native American tribes formed a confederation to keep settlers from taking their lands.

Declaration of Independence (deh-kluh-RAY-shun OF in-dee-PEN-dens)
The Declaration of Independence is a document that was written in 1776. It announced the independence of the United States from Great Britain.

economy (ee-KON-uh-mee)
An economy is the way money is earned and spent. Southerners believed that ending slavery would ruin their economy.

federal (FED-er-ul)
Federal means having to do with the central government of the United States, rather than a state or city government. Some states gave up their western lands to the federal government in the 1780s.

inauguration (ih-nawg-yuh-RAY-shun)
An inauguration is the ceremony that takes place when a new president begins a term. The day of Harrison's inauguration was cold and wet.

legislature (LEJ-ih-slay-chur)
A legislature is the part of a government that makes laws. Harrison's father was a member of the Virginia legislature.

minister (MIN-eh-stir)
A minister is a person who is in charge of one part of the government. The minister to Colombia is in charge of U.S. relations with that country.

negotiate (nee-GOH-shee-ayt)
If people negotiate, they talk things over and try to come to an agreement. Harrison negotiated a treaty with Native Americans in 1809.

patriot (PAY-tree-ut)
A patriot is someone who loves their country so much, they are willing to fight for it. Benjamin Harrison was a patriot.

pneumonia (noo-MOH-nyuh)
Pneumonia is a disease that causes swelling of the lungs, high fever, and difficulty breathing. President Harrison died of pneumonia.

**political party
(puh-LIT-ih-kul PAR-tee)**
A political party is a group of people who share similar ideas about how to run a government. Harrison was a member of the Democratic political party at one time.

politician (pawl-ih-TISH-un)
A politician is a person who holds an office in government. Harrison wanted to be a politician like his father.

principles (PRIN-sih-puls)
Principles are a people's basic beliefs, or what they believe to be right and true. Harrison hoped the president who followed him would understand the principles of the U.S. government.

recruit (ree-KREWT)
When people recruit others, they convince them to join a group. Harrison recruited men to the army.

representative (rep-ree-ZEN-tuh-tiv)
A representative is someone who attends a meeting, having agreed to speak or act for others. Harrison was the Northwest Territory's representative in the U.S. Congress in 1798.

siege (SEEJ)
If people or places are under siege, they have been surrounded or captured. The British put Harrison's men under siege during the War of 1812.

territory (TAIR-ih-tor-ee)
A territory is a land or region, especially land that belongs to a government. A new law in 1787 created the Northwest Territory.

traditions (tra-DIH-shunz)
Traditions are customs handed down from one generation to the next. Tenskwatawa tried to help Native Americans bring back their traditions.

Our PRESIDENTS

President	Birthplace	Life Span	Presidency	Political Party	First Lady
George Washington	Virginia	1732–1799	1789–1797	None	Martha Dandridge Custis Washington
John Adams	Massachusetts	1735–1826	1797–1801	Federalist	Abigail Smith Adams
Thomas Jefferson	Virginia	1743–1826	1801–1809	Democratic-Republican	widower
James Madison	Virginia	1751–1836	1809–1817	Democratic Republican	Dolley Payne Todd Madison
James Monroe	Virginia	1758–1831	1817–1825	Democratic Republican	Elizabeth Kortright Monroe
John Quincy Adams	Massachusetts	1767–1848	1825–1829	Democratic-Republican	Louisa Johnson Adams
Andrew Jackson	South Carolina	1767–1845	1829–1837	Democrat	widower
Martin Van Buren	New York	1782–1862	1837–1841	Democrat	widower
William H. Harrison	Virginia	1773–1841	1841	Whig	Anna Symmes Harrison
John Tyler	Virginia	1790–1862	1841–1845	Whig	Letitia Christian Tyler / Julia Gardiner Tyler
James K. Polk	North Carolina	1795–1849	1845–1849	Democrat	Sarah Childress Polk

President	Birthplace	Life Span	Presidency	Political Party	First Lady
Zachary Taylor	Virginia	1784–1850	1849–1850	Whig	Margaret Mackall Smith Taylor
Millard Fillmore	New York	1800–1874	1850–1853	Whig	Abigail Powers Fillmore
Franklin Pierce	New Hampshire	1804–1869	1853–1857	Democrat	Jane Means Appleton Pierce
James Buchanan	Pennsylvania	1791–1868	1857–1861	Democrat	never married
Abraham Lincoln	Kentucky	1809–1865	1861–1865	Republican	Mary Todd Lincoln
Andrew Johnson	North Carolina	1808–1875	1865–1869	Democrat	Eliza McCardle Johnson
Ulysses S. Grant	Ohio	1822–1885	1869–1877	Republican	Julia Dent Grant
Rutherford B. Hayes	Ohio	1822–1893	1877–1881	Republican	Lucy Webb Hayes
James A. Garfield	Ohio	1831–1881	1881	Republican	Lucretia Rudolph Garfield
Chester A. Arthur	Vermont	1829–1886	1881–1885	Republican	widower
Grover Cleveland	New Jersey	1837–1908	1885–1889	Democrat	Frances Folsom Cleveland

Our PRESIDENTS

President	Birthplace	Life Span	Presidency	Political Party	First Lady
Benjamin Harrison	Ohio	1833–1901	1889–1893	Republican	Caroline Scott Harrison
Grover Cleveland	New Jersey	1837–1908	1893–1897	Democrat	Frances Folsom Cleveland
William McKinley	Ohio	1843–1901	1897–1901	Republican	Ida Saxton McKinley
Theodore Roosevelt	New York	1858–1919	1901–1909	Republican	Edith Kermit Carow Roosevelt
William H. Taft	Ohio	1857–1930	1909–1913	Republican	Helen Herron Taft
Woodrow Wilson	Virginia	1856–1924	1913–1921	Democrat	Ellen L. Axson Wilson Edith Bolling Galt Wilson
Warren G. Harding	Ohio	1865–1923	1921–1923	Republican	Florence Kling De Wolfe Harding
Calvin Coolidge	Vermont	1872–1933	1923–1929	Republican	Grace Goodhue Coolidge
Herbert C. Hoover	Iowa	1874–1964	1929–1933	Republican	Lou Henry Hoover
Franklin D. Roosevelt	New York	1882–1945	1933–1945	Democrat	Anna Eleanor Roosevelt Roosevelt
Harry S. Truman	Missouri	1884–1972	1945–1953	Democrat	Elizabeth Wallace Truman

Our PRESIDENTS

President	Birthplace	Life Span	Presidency	Political Party	First Lady
Dwight D. Eisenhower	Texas	1890–1969	1953–1961	Republican	Mary "Mamie" Doud Eisenhower
John F. Kennedy	Massachusetts	1917–1963	1961–1963	Democrat	Jacqueline Bouvier Kennedy
Lyndon B. Johnson	Texas	1908–1973	1963–1969	Democrat	Claudia Alta Taylor Johnson
Richard M. Nixon	California	1913–1994	1969–1974	Republican	Thelma Catherine Ryan Nixon
Gerald Ford	Nebraska	1913–	1974–1977	Republican	Elizabeth "Betty" Bloomer Warren Ford
James Carter	Georgia	1924–	1977–1981	Democrat	Rosalynn Smith Carter
Ronald Reagan	Illinois	1911–	1981–1989	Republican	Nancy Davis Reagan
George Bush	Massachusetts	1924–	1989–1993	Republican	Barbara Pierce Bush
William Clinton	Arkansas	1946–	1993–2001	Democrat	Hillary Rodham Clinton
George W. Bush	Connecticut	1946–	2001–	Republican	Laura Welch Bush

Qualifications

To run for president, a candidate must
- be at least 35 years old
- be a citizen who was born in the United States
- have lived in the United States for 14 years

Term of Office

A president's term of office is four years. No president can stay in office for more than two terms.

Election Date

The presidential election takes place every four years on the first Tuesday of November.

Inauguration Date

Presidents are inaugurated on January 20.

Oath of Office

I do solemnly swear I will faithfully execute the office of the President of the United States and will to the best of my ability preserve, protect, and defend the Constitution of the United States.

Write a Letter to the President

One of the best things about being a U.S. citizen is that Americans get to participate in their government. They can speak out if they feel government leaders aren't doing their jobs. They can also praise leaders who are going the extra mile. Do you have something you'd like the president to do? Should the president worry more about the environment and encourage people to recycle? Should the government spend more money on our schools? You can write a letter to the president to say how you feel!

1600 Pennsylvania Avenue
Washington, D.C. 20500

You can even send an e-mail to: president@whitehouse.gov

For Further INFORMATION

Internet Sites

Find out about William Henry Harrison's papers at the Indiana State Library:
http://www.indianahistory.org/whh.htm

Visit Berkeley Plantation, Harrison's birthplace, and other plantations in Virginia:
http://www.berkeleyplantation.com/
http://www.jamesriverplantations.org

Read what Harrison wrote about the Battle of Tippecanoe:
http://www.prairienet.org/~pcollins/whh.html

Find out about Harrison's time as governor of Indiana:
http://www.statelib.lib.in.us/www/ihb/harrison.html

Find out about Harrison's political career in Ohio:
http://www.ohiobio.org/harrison.htm

Learn more about Harrison's grandson, who also became president, at the Benjamin Harrison Home:
http://www.surf-ici.com/harrison/

Learn more about all the presidents and visit the White House:
http://www.whitehouse.gov/WH/glimpse/presidents/html/presidents.html
http://www.thepresidency.org/presinfo.htm
http://www.americanpresidents.org/

Books

Cwiklik, Robert, and W. David Baird. *Tecumseh: Shawnee Rebel* (North American Indians of Achievement). Broomall, PA: Chelsea House, 1993.

Feinberg, Barbara Silberdick. *America's First Ladies.* New York: Franklin Watts, 1998.

Hakim, Joy. *From Colonies to Country.* New York: Oxford University Press, 1993.

Marrin, Albert. *1812: The War Nobody Won.* New York: Atheneum, 1985.

Rubel, David. *Scholastic Encyclopedia of the Presidents and Their Times.* New York: Scholastic, 1994.